Paget Surname

Ireland: 1600s to 1900s

From Ireland Church Records of Baptism, Marriage and Death

Comprised of Roman Catholic and Church of Ireland Records

From Counties Carlow, Cork, Kerry and Dublin City

Compiled by **Donovan Hurst**

March 29, 2013

Dedication

This work is dedicated to all of those that came before us and shaped our lives to make us the people that we are today.

Table of Contents

Introduction

This is a compilation of individuals who have the surname of Paget that lived in the country of Ireland from the 1600s to the 1900s. I have placed each entry into one of four categories: Families, Individual Births/Baptisms, Individual Burials, and Individual Marriages. If a marriage entry primarily concerns an Individual Paget whom is female, then I have placed that entry under the category of Individual Marriages. If a marriage entry primarily concerns an Individual Paget whom is male, then I have placed that entry under the category of Families. Images of many of these listings are available at http://churchrecords.irishgenealogy.ie/churchrecords/.

To help guide the reader of this work, the format of this book is as follows:

- Main Family Entry (Husband and Wife) (Father and Mother)

  o Child of Main Family Entry, including Spouse(s) when available

    ▪ Grandchild of Main Family Entry, including Spouse(s) when available

    • Great-Grandchild of Main Family Entry, including Spouse(s) when available

(**Bolded Text**) following any entry includes any additional information such as Residence(s), Occupation(s), Signature(s), etc. when available.

Hurst

Some of the fonts used in this work symbolizes Celtic writing. The traditional letters, numbers, and punctuation marks and their Celtic counterparts are as follows:

Traditional Letters (Uppercase & Lowercase)

A a B b C c D d E f G g H h I i J j K k L l M m N n O o P p Q q R r S s T t U u V v W w X x Y y Z z

Celtic Letters (Uppercase & Lowercase)

A a B b C c D ð E e F f G g H h I i J j K k L l M m

N n O o P p Q q R r S s T t U u V v W w X x Y y Z z

Traditional Numbers

1 2 3 4 5 6 7 8 9 10

Celtic Numbers

1 2 3 4 5 6 7 8 9 10

Traditional Punctuation

. , : ' " & - ( )

Celtic Punctuation

. , : ' " & - ( )

Parish Churches

Carlow (Church of Ireland)

Carlow Parish.

Dublin (Church of Ireland)

Arbour Hill Barracks Parish, Irishtown Parish, Leeson Park Parish, North Strand Parish, Rotunda Chapel Parish, South Dublin Union Parish, St. Audoen Parish, St. George Parish, St. John Parish, St. Mark Parish, St. Mary Parish, St. Michan Parish, St. Nicholas Within Parish, St. Nicholas Without Parish, St. Paul Parish, St. Peter Parish, and St. Stephen Parish.

Dublin (Roman Catholic or RC)

St. Agatha Parish, St. Catherine Parish, St. Lawrence Parish, St. Mary, Pro Cathedral Parish, St. Michan Parish, and St. Nicholas Parish.

Families

- Alexander Paget & Esther Branagan

  - Christopher Paget – b. 24 Jan 1866, bapt. 7 Feb 1866 (Baptism, **St. Mary, Pro Cathedral Parish (RC)**)

Alexander Paget (father):

Residence - 20 Lower Temple Street - February 7, 1866

- Benjamin Paget & Mary Paget

  - Richard Paget – bapt. 6 Nov 1761 (Baptism, **St. Mary Parish**)

- Edward Paget & Harriet Unknown

  - Patrick Lewis Cole Paget – b. 10 Feb 1820, bapt. 29 Feb 1820 (Baptism, **St. Peter Parish**)

Edward Paget (father):

Social Status - Sir

Harriet Unknown (mother):

Social Status - Lady

- Frederick Paget & Sarah Paget

  - Frederick John Paget – b. 15 Dec 1887, bapt. 13 Jan 1888 (Baptism, **Arbour Hill Barracks Parish**)

  - Muriel Grace Paget – b. 12 Oct 1895, bapt. 6 Nov 1895 (Baptism, **Arbour Hill Barracks Parish**)

Hurst

Frederick Paget (father):

Residence - 11 Findlater Street - January 13, 1888

Warder's Quarters, Arbour Hill - November 6, 1895

Occupation - Military Prison Warder - January 13, 1888

Warder, Military Prison - November 6, 1895

- Gulielmo Paget & Teresa Walsh
  - Gulielmo John Paget – b. 14 Jun 1888, bapt. 22 Jun 1888 (Baptism, **St. Agatha Parish** (RC))

Gulielmo Paget (father):

Residence - 35 Clarence Street - June 22, 1888

- Henry Paget & Anne Paget, bur. 19 Dec 1683 (Burial, **St. Michan Parish**)
  - Thomas Paget – bur. 1 Jul 1678 (Burial, **St. Michan Parish**)
  - John Paget – bur. 9 Dec 1680 (Burial, **St. Michan Parish**)

Henry Paget (father):

Occupation - Ensign - July 1, 1678

Lieutenant - December 9, 1680

December 19, 1683

- James Paget & Catherine Benson – 17 Oct 1829 (Marriage, **St. Peter Parish**)

James Paget (husband):

Residence - Dominick Street - October 17, 1829

Paget Surname Ireland: 1600s to 1900s

Catherine Benson (wife):

Residence - Baggot Street - October 17, 1829

Occupation - Spinster - October 17, 1829

Wedding Witnesses:

Charles Benson & Maureen Mahon

- James Paget & Jane Unknown
  - Mary Paget – bapt. 25 Oct 1764 (Baptism, **St. Peter Parish**)
- James Paget & Jane Caroline Knox – 19 Aug 1857 (Marriage, **St. Mark Parish**)

Signatures:

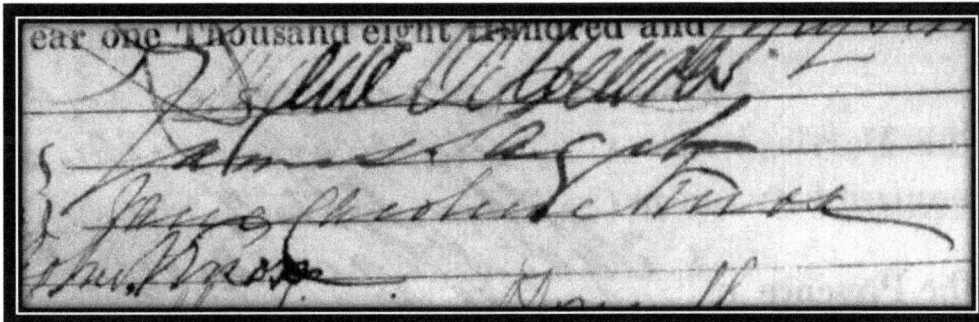

James Paget (husband):

Residence - St. Mark Parish - August 19, 1857

Jane Caroline Knox (wife):

Residence - Crossmolina Parish, Co. Mayo - August 19, 1857

Hurst

Wedding Witnesses:

John Knox & George Clendinning O'Donnell

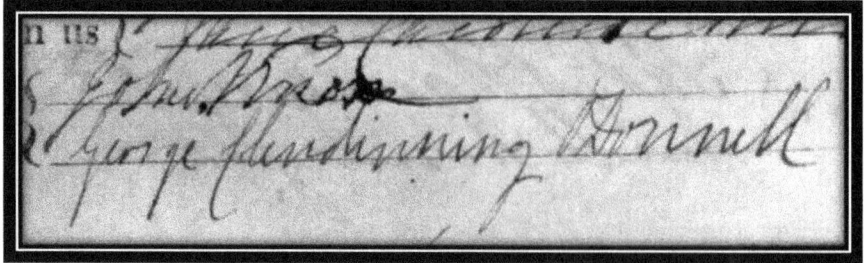

Signatures:

- James Paget & Hannah Paget

  - Elizabeth Paget – b. 22 Feb 1855, bapt. 2 Mar 1855 (Baptism, **St. Mark Parish**)

James Paget (father):

Residence - 2 Erne Place - March 2, 1855

Occupation - Farmer - March 2, 1855

- James Paget & Margaret Paget

  - Benjamin Paget – bapt. 29 Oct 1785 (Baptism, **St. Mary Parish**)

  - Mary Paget – bapt. 16 Dec 1787 (Baptism, **St. Mary Parish**)

  - Thomas Paget – bapt. 30 Dec 1797 (Baptism, **St. Mary Parish**)

James Paget (father):

Residence - Marlborough Street - December 30, 1797

Paget Surname Ireland: 1600s to 1900s

- John Paget & Alice McCord

  - James Paget – bapt. 15 Jun 1779 (Baptism, **St. Michan Parish (RC)**)

  - Elizabeth Paget – bapt. 13 Jul 1783 (Baptism, **St. Michan Parish (RC)**)

  - Thomas Paget – bapt. 10 Apr 1785 (Baptism, **St. Michan Parish (RC)**)

  - Alice Paget – bapt. 17 Jul 1787 (Baptism, **St. Michan Parish (RC)**)

- John Paget & Anne Unknown

  - John Paget – bapt. 1 Sep 1752 (Baptism, **St. Michan Parish (RC)**)

- John Paget & Elizabeth Baile – 12 Oct 1736 (Marriage, **St. Mary Parish**)

  - John Paget – bapt. 9 Aug 1737 (Baptism, **St. Mary Parish**), bur. 25 Aug 1738 (Burial, **St. Mary Parish**)

  - Elizabeth Paget – bapt. 29 Apr 1739 (Baptism, **St. Mary Parish**)

  - Frances Paget – b. 23 Mar 1741, bapt. 14 Apr 1741 (Baptism, **St. Mary Parish**)

  - Mary Paget – b. 29 Mar 1742, bapt. 9 Apr 1742 (Baptism, **St. Mary Parish**)

- John Paget & Mary Murphy – 28 May 1843 (Marriage, **St. Nicholas Parish (RC)**)

Wedding Witnesses:

John Paget & Edward Sherwood

- John Paget & Unknown

  - Richard Paget – bur. 8 May 1676 (Burial, **St. Nicholas Within Parish**)

- Noble Paget & Unknown

  - James Sutcliffe Paget, b. 1834, bur. 25 Oct 1894 (Burial, **St. George Parish**) & Frances Hamilton – 2 Dec 1856 (Marriage, **St. Peter Parish**)

Hurst

Signature:

Signatures (Marriage):

James Sutcliffe Paget (son):

    Residence - Killucan Rectory Carrich on Shannon - December 2, 1856

        13 Drumcondra Road - before October 25, 1894

    Occupation - Clerk in Holy Orders - December 2, 1856

    Age at Death - 60 years

Frances Hamilton, daughter of William Hamilton (daughter-in-law):

    Residence - Caravetra Lodge, Clover, Co. Cavan - December 2, 1856

William Hamilton (father):

    Occupation - Lieutenant in the Army

Noble Paget (father):

    Occupation - Land Agent

Paget Surname Ireland: 1600s to 1900s

Wedding Witnesses:

Thomas Dawson & John Richardson

Signatures:

- Richard Paget & Elizabeth Paget

  o Margaret Paget – bapt. 7 Sep 1714 (Baptism, **St. Mary Parish**)

- Richard Paget & Unknown

  o Margaret Paget – bur. 24 May 1703 (Burial, **St. Nicholas Within Parish**)

- Robert Paget & Bridget Unknown

  o Robert Paget – bapt. 7 Oct 1822 (Baptism, **St. Mary, Pro Cathedral Parish (RC)**)

Robert Paget (father):

Residence - Britain Street - October 7, 1822

- Robert Paget & Elizabeth Paget

  o Isabel Paget & James Heatty – 20 Sep 1897 (Marriage, **North Strand Parish**)

Signatures:

Isabel Paget (daughter):

Residence - 12 Dunne Street, North William Street - September 20, 1897

James Heatty, son of William Heatty (son-in-law):

Residence - 3 Jane Place, Seville Place - September 20, 1897

Occupation - Coal Porter - September 20, 1897

William Heatty (father):

Occupation - Farmer

Robert Paget (father):

Occupation - Bottle Maker

Wedding Witnesses:

Harriet Filgate & James Rothwell

Signatures:

- o   Robert Paget – b. 26 Dec 1881, bapt. 27 Jan 1882 (Baptism, Irishtown Parish)

Robert Paget (father):

Residence - Ring's End - January 27, 1882

Occupation - Glass Blower - January 27, 1882

Paget Surname Ireland: 1600s to 1900s

- Robert Paget & Margaret Egnan, d. bef. 6 Aug 1880

  o John Patrick Paget, b. 23 Nov 1857, bapt. 6 Aug 1880 (Baptism, **St. Lawrence Parish** (RC)) & Catherine Macken – 22 Aug 1880 (Marriage, **St. Lawrence Parish** (RC))

John Patrick Paget (son):

Residence - 6 Williams Place - August 6, 1880

August 22, 1880

Catherine Macken, daughter of John Macken & Agnes Unknown (daughter-in-law):

Residence - 19 Lower Jane Place - August 22, 1880

Wedding Witnesses:

Lawrence Kelly & Esther Tyrrell

Robert Paget (father):

Residence - 6 Williams Place - August 6, 1880

- Robert Paget & Margaret Reny

  o Isabel Paget – b. 11 Feb 1854, bapt. 20 Feb 1854 (Baptism, **St. Lawrence Parish** (RC))

Robert Paget (father):

Residence - 5 Emerald Street - February 20, 1854

- Stewart Henry Paget & Unknown

  o Arthur Cecil Henry Paget & Sophia Caroline Bushe – 16 Jun 1870 (Marriage, **St. Stephen Parish**)

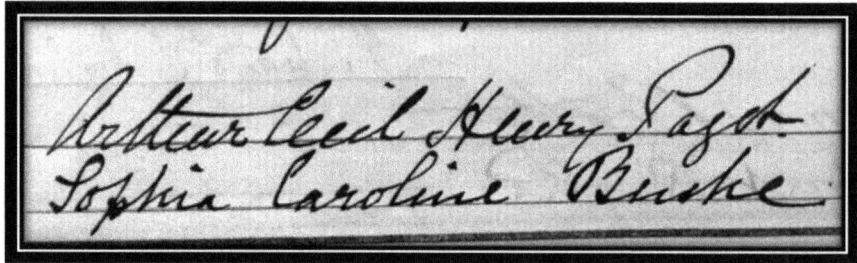

Signatures:

Arthur Cecil Henry Paget (son):

Residence - 86 Lower Baggot Street - June 16, 1870

Occupation - Lieutenant R N [Royal Navy] - June 16, 1870

Sophia Caroline Bushe, daughter of Charles Bushe (daughter-in-law):

Residence - 86 Lower Baggot Street - June 16, 1870

Charles Bushe (father):

Occupation - Clerk in Holy Orders

Stewart Henry Paget (father):

Residence - Esquire

Paget Surname Ireland: 1600s to 1900s

Wedding Witnesses:

William Sydney Hilton Jolliffe & Charles Percy Bushe

Signatures:

- Thomas Paget & Anne Sarah Westland – 31 Aug 1728 (Marrige, **St. Michan Parish**)

    o   Mary Paget – bapt. 28 Aug 1729 (Baptism, **St. Mary Parish**)

    o   Elizabeth Paget – bapt. 15 Dec 1730 (Baptism, **St. Mary Parish**)

    o   Martha Paget – bapt. 13 Feb 1731 (Baptism, **St. Mary Parish**)

    o   Thomas Paget – bapt. 29 Jan 1733 (Baptism, **St. Mary Parish**)

    o   Anne Paget – bapt. 30 May 1735 (Baptism, **St. Mary Parish**)

Thomas Paget (father):

Occupation - Gentleman - August 31, 1728

- Thomas Paget & Jane Paget

    o   Joseph Paget – bapt. 1 Mar 1789 (Baptism, **St. Mary Parish**)

    o   Jane Paget – bapt. 27 Mar 1791 (Baptism, **St. Mary Parish**)

Thomas Paget (father):

Residence - Liffey Street - March 1, 1789

Hurst

Lower Ormond Quay - March 27, 1791

- Thomas Paget & Mary Kane

  - Charles Paget – b. 4 Apr 1856, bapt. 14 Apr 1856 (Baptism, **St. Mary, Pro Cathedral Parish (RC)**)

Thomas Paget (father):

Residence - Mecklenburgh Street - April 14, 1856

- Thomas Paget & Mary Unknown

  - Catherine Paget – bapt. 7 Sep 1832 (Baptism, **St. Mary, Pro Cathedral Parish (RC)**)

  - Thomas Paget – bapt. 29 Oct 1834 (Baptism, **St. Mary, Pro Cathedral Parish (RC)**)

  - Margaret Paget – bapt. 22 May 1839 (Baptism, **St. Mary, Pro Cathedral Parish (RC)**)

- Unknown Paget & Jane Paget

  - Henry Paget – b. 3 Dec 1888, bapt. 7 Dec 1888 (Baptism, **Rotunda Chapel Parish**)

Jane Paget (mother):

Residence - V. Ward, Rotunda Hospital & 3 Cowley Place - December 7, 1888

Occupation - General Servant - December 7, 1888

- Unknown Paget & Janet Paget

  - George Paget – b. 1895, bapt. 25 Jul 1895 (Baptism, **South Dublin Union Parish**)

Janet Paget (mother):

Relationship Status - not married

Paget Surname Ireland: 1600s to 1900s

- Unknown Paget & Unknown

  o James H. Paget

Signature:

- Unknown Paget & Unknown

  o Thomas Paget – bur. 16 Mar 1689 (Burial, **St. Audoen Parish**)

- Unknown Paget & Unknown

  o Lydia Paget – bur. 14 Dec 1703 (Burial, **St. Nicholas Within Parish**)

- William Paget & Bridget McGann

  o William Paget – b. 28 Oct 1864, bapt. 23 Nov 1864 (Baptism, **St. Nicholas Parish (RC)**)

William Paget (father):

Residence - 10 Upper Kevin Street - November 23, 1864

- William Paget & Frances Paget

  o William Henry Paget – b. 13 Mar 1829, bapt. 13 Mar 1829 (Baptism, **St. George Parish**)

William Henry Paget (father):

Residence - 19 Eccles Street - March 13, 1829

- William Paget & Mary Smyth

  o Mark Paget – bapt. 1 Aug 1803 (Baptism, **St. Catherine Parish (RC)**)

- William Paget & Teresa Walsh

  - Thomas Paget – b. 20 Jul 1885, bapt. 29 Jul 1885 (Baptism, **St. Mary, Pro Cathedral Parish (RC)**)

  - Isabel Paget – b. 2 Mar 1891, bapt. 9 Mar 1891 (Baptism, **St. Mary, Pro Cathedral Parish (RC)**)

William Paget (father):

Residence - 8 Upper Buckingham Street - July 29, 1885

Rotunda - March 9, 1891

- William Paget & Unknown

  - John Paget – bur. 17 Nov 1668 (Burial, **St. Michan Parish**)

William Paget (father):

Occupation - Soldier - November 17, 1668

- William Paget & Unknown

  - John Paget – bur. 5 Sep 1691 (Burial, **St. Nicholas Within Parish**)

- William Paget & Unknown

  - Unknown Paget – bapt. 5 Jan 1729 (Baptism, **St. John Parish**)

- William Paget & Unknown

  - William Byerly Paget & Elizabeth Crowe – 4 Sep 1872 (Marriage, **St. Stephen Parish**)

Signatures:

Paget Surname Ireland: 1600s to 1900s

- Gertrude Mary Paget – b. 10 Jun 1873, bapt. 9 Jul 1873 (Baptism, **Leeson Park Parish**)

William Byerly Paget (son):

Residence - Loughborough, Leicestershire, England - September 4, 1872

Southfield Loughborough, Leicestershire, England - July 9, 1873

Occupation - Esquire - September 4, 1872

Gentleman - July 9, 1873

Elizabeth Crowe, daughter of Thomas Crowe (daughter-in-law):

Residence - 14 Merrion Square East - September 4, 1872

Thomas Crowe (father):

Occupation - Esquire

William Paget (father):

Occupation - Esquire

Wedding Witnesses:

Thomas Crowe & Francis Parker

Signatures:

Individual Baptisms/Births

- George Paget – bapt. 2 Nov 1746 (Baptism, **St. Paul Parish**)

George Paget (child):

Age at Baptism - child

Individual Burials

- Dorothy Paget – bur. 15 Dec 1709 (Burial, **St. Nicholas Without Parish**)

- James Paget – b. 1757, bur. 1 Apr 1837 (Burial, **St. Mary Parish**)

James Paget (deceased):

　　Residence - Dorset Street - before April 1, 1837

　　Age at Death - 80 years

- Lydia Paget – bur. 14 Dec 1705 (Burial, **St. Nicholas Without Parish**)

- Margaret Paget – bur. 16 Mar 1707 (Burial, **St. Nicholas Within Parish**)

- Margaret Paget – bur. 16 Mar 1708 (Burial, **St. Nicholas Without Parish**)

- Richard Paget – bur. 2 Jan 1725 (Burial, **St. Nicholas Within Parish**)

- Richard Paget – bur. Jan 1729 (Burial, **St. Nicholas Without Parish**)

- Thomas Paget – bur. 2 Oct 1735 (Burial, **St. Audoen Parish**)

Thomas Paget (deceased):

　　Residence - Mary Street - before October 2, 1735

- Unknown Paget – bur. 20 Aug 1745 (Burial, **St. Mary Parish**)

Unknown Paget (deceased):

　　Age at Death - child

Hurst

- Unknown Paget (Miss) – bur. 14 Apr 1746 (Burial, **St. Mary Parish**)

- Unknown Paget (Miss) – bur. 12 Mar 1806 (Burial, **St. Mary Parish**)

Unknown Paget (Miss) (deceased):

Residence- Stafford Street - before March 12, 1806

- Unknown Paget (Miss) – bur. 14 Sep 1820 (Burial, **St. Mary Parish**)

Unknown Paget (Miss) (deceased):

Residence - Dorset Street - before September 14, 1820

- Unknown Paget (Miss) – b. 1776, bur. 25 Apr 1824 (Burial, **St. Mary Parish**)

Unknown Paget (Miss) (deceased):

Age at Death - 48 years

- Unknown Paget (Miss) – b. 1756, bur. 13 Dec 1837 (Burial, **St. Mary Parish**)

Unknown Paget (Miss) (deceased):

Residence - Dorset Street - before December 13, 1837

Age at Death - 81 years

- Unknown Paget (Mr.) – bur. 20 Jul 1746 (Burial, **St. Mary Parish**)

- Unknown Paget (Mrs.) – bur. 30 Jun 1727 (Burial, **St. Nicholas Within Parish**) (Burial, **St. Nicholas Without Parish**)

Paget Surname Ireland: 1600s to 1900s

- Unknown Paget (Mrs.) – bur. 25 Apr 1738 (Burial, **St. Audoen Parish**)

Unknown Paget (Mrs.) (deceased):

Residence - Bull Lane - before April 25, 1738

- Unknown Paget (Mrs.) – bur. 7 Jul 1789 (Burial, **St. Mary Parish**)

Unknown Paget (Mrs.) (deceased):

Residence - Stafford Street - before July 7, 1789

- Westland Paget – bur. 27 Feb 1737 (Burial, **St. Audoen Parish**)

Westland Paget (deceased):

Residence - Herey S. - before February 27, 1737

- William Paget – bur. 26 Sep 1724 (Burial, **St. Nicholas Within Parish**) (Burial, **St. Nicholas Without Parish**)

- William Paget – bur. 17 Jun 1788 (Burial, **St. Paul Parish**)

Individual Marriages

- Angelica Paget & Unknown Crump – 18 Dec 1749 (Marriage, **Carlow Parish**)

Unknown Crump (husband):

Occupation - Doctor - December 18, 1749

- Margaret Paget & Christopher Donnelly
  - John Donnelly – b. 16 Oct 1872, bapt. 21 Oct 1872 (Baptism, **St. Lawrence Parish** (RC))

Christopher Donnelly (father):

Residence - 3 William Place - October 21, 1872

Paget Surname Ireland: 1600s to 1900s

Name Variations

Includes Latin and Abbreviated forms of names found in the original documents.

Abigail = Abigale, Abigall

Anne = Ann, Anna, Annae

Bartholomew = Barth, Bartholmeus, Bartholomeo

Bridget = Birgis, Brigid, Brigida, Bridgit

Catherine = Catharine, Catharina, Catharinae, Catherina, Cath, Catha, Cathae, Cathe, Cathn, Kate

Charles = Carolus, Charls, Chas

Christopher = Christoph

Daniel = Danielem, Danielis

Edmund = Edmond

Edward = Ed, Edwd

Eleanor = Eleo, Eleonora, Elinor, Ellenor

Elizabeth = Betty, Elisa, Elisabeth, Eliz, Eliza, Elizab, Elizh, Elizth

Ellen = Elena, Ellena

Emily = Emilia

Esther = Essie, Ester

Francis = Fransicum

George = Geo, Georg, Georgius

Grace = Gratiae

Gulielmo = Guil, Guillelmi, Gulielmum, Guillelmus, Gulmi

Helen = Helena

Paget Surname Ireland: 1600s to 1900s

Honor = Hanora, Honora

James = Jacobi, Jacobus, Jas

Jane = Joanna

Jeanne = Jeannae, Joannae

Joan = Johanna, Joney

John = Jno, Joannem, Joannes, Johannis

Joseph = Jos

Juliana = Julian

Leticia = Letitia, Lettice, Letticia

Lewis = Louis

Luke = Lucas

Margaret = Margarita, Margaritae, Margeret, Marget, Margt

Martha = Marthae

Mary = Maria, My

Mary Anne = Marianna, Marianne, Maryanne

Michael = Michaelis, Michl

Patrick = Pat, Patt, Patk, Patricii, Patricius

Peter = Petri

Richard = Ricardi, Ricardus, Rich, Richd

Robert = Roberti

Rose = Rosa, Rosae

Thomas = Thom, Thomae, Thoms, Thos, Ths

Timothy = Timotheus, Timy

William = Wil, Will, Willm, Wm

Notes

Notes

Notes

Notes

Notes

Notes

Index

Paget Surname Ireland: 1600s to 1900s

Paget

Births

⟨ R ⟩

⟨ S ⟩

U

W

About The Author

Donovan Hurst graduated from San Diego State University with a Bachelor of Arts in the major field of studies of History and a minor in the field of studies of Anthropology. He is a current member of The General Society of Mayflower Descendants and has been conducting genealogical research for over 10 years tracing back his ancestors to their ancestral homelands in Denmark, England, France, Germany, Ireland, Norway, and Scotland.